Denver Broncos

BY
ZACH WYNER

AV² provides enriched content that supplements and complements this book. Weigl's AV² books strive to create inspired learning and engage young minds in a total learning experience.

Your AV² Media Enhanced books come alive with...

Audio
Listen to sections of the book read aloud.

Key Words
Study vocabulary, and complete a matching word activity.

Video
Watch informative video clips.

Quizzes
Test your knowledge.

Embedded Weblinks
Gain additional information for research.

Slide Show
View images and captions, and prepare a presentation.

Try This!
Complete activities and hands-on experiments.

... and much, much more!

Go to **www.av2books.com**, and enter this book's unique code.

BOOK CODE

U 5 3 1 0

AV² by Weigl brings you media enhanced books that support active learning.

Published by AV² by Weigl
350 5th Avenue, 59th Floor
New York, NY 10118
Websites: www.av2books.com   www.weigl.com

Library of Congress Control Number: 2014930779

ISBN 978-1-4896-0818-5 (hardcover)
ISBN 978-1-4896-0820-8 (single-user eBook)
ISBN 978-1-4896-0821-5 (multi-user eBook)

Printed in the United States of America in North Mankato, Minnesota
2 3 4 5 6 7 8 9 0 18 17 16 15 14

112014
WEP211114

Project Coordinator Aaron Carr
Art Director Terry Paulhus

Photo Credits
Every reasonable effort has been made to trace ownership and to obtain permission to reprint copyright material. The publishers would be pleased to have any errors or omissions brought to their attention so that they may be corrected in subsequent printings.

Weigl acknowledges Getty Images as its primary image supplier for this title.

Denver Broncos

CONTENTS

Introduction

Denver, Colorado, is known throughout the National Football League (NFL) as the city opposing teams least want to visit. This is because visiting players struggle to breathe in the thinner air found at 5,000 feet (1,524 meters) above sea level. Meanwhile, the Denver Broncos and their historically high-scoring offense light up the scoreboard to the delight of one of the most raucous crowds in the NFL.

The people of Denver have known disappointment. In fact, it took the Broncos 17 long years just to qualify for the playoffs. The team's fortunes finally changed with the arrival of the "Orange Crush" defense. This was the nickname given to the dominant defensive unit of the 1970s because of the Broncos' orange home jerseys and the popular soft drink, Orange Crush.

In 1967, the Broncos held a contest for the public to design a new logo. A Denver local named Edwin Guy Taylor won with his simple "D" design.

By the time a quarterback named John Elway was drafted in 1983, Broncos fans were used to winning. Now, with two Super Bowl titles under their belt, every Broncos season begins with dreams of a championship.

Peyton Manning's 55 touchdown passes in 2013 shattered Tom Brady's single season mark of 50 touchdown throws in 2007.

BRONCOS
DENVER

Stadium Sports Authority Field at Mile High

Division American Football Conference (AFC) West

Head coach John Fox

Location Denver, Colorado

Super Bowl titles 1997, 1998

Nicknames Orange Crush

20
Playoff Appearances

2
Super Bowl Championships

13
Division Championships

History

ON A ROLL

The Broncos lost their first four **SUPER BOWLS** before winning **BACK-TO-BACK TITLES** in 1997 and 1998.

Floyd Little played all nine of his professional seasons with the Denver Broncos.

In 1960, the Denver Broncos were **charter members** of the **American Football League (AFL)**. The AFL grew and became a part of the older and more established NFL, but the Broncos still struggled. When it looked as though the Broncos might not survive, the team's first star, Floyd "The Franchise" Little, went door-to-door, selling season tickets, in order to keep the Broncos in Denver.

Then, in 1977, the Broncos' "Orange Crush" defense lifted them into the national spotlight. While the rest of the country was just getting to know the franchise, Denver fans had been supporting their team for years. Back in 1970, the Broncos had begun a string of sold out home games that continues to this day. Between 1977 and 2012, the Broncos won 11 AFC West Division titles. Much of their success was due to one man. Drafted in 1983, John Elway quarterbacked Denver to five Super Bowl appearances in his 16-year hall of fame career. In 1997, he and running back Terrell Davis led the Broncos to their first of two Super Bowl victories.

In 2012, the Broncos signed future hall of fame quarterback Peyton Manning. In his first season, Manning led the Broncos to 13 wins and a division title. In 2013, he led an all-out assault on the record books.

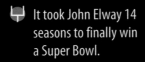 It took John Elway 14 seasons to finally win a Super Bowl.

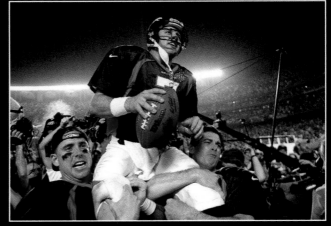

The Stadium

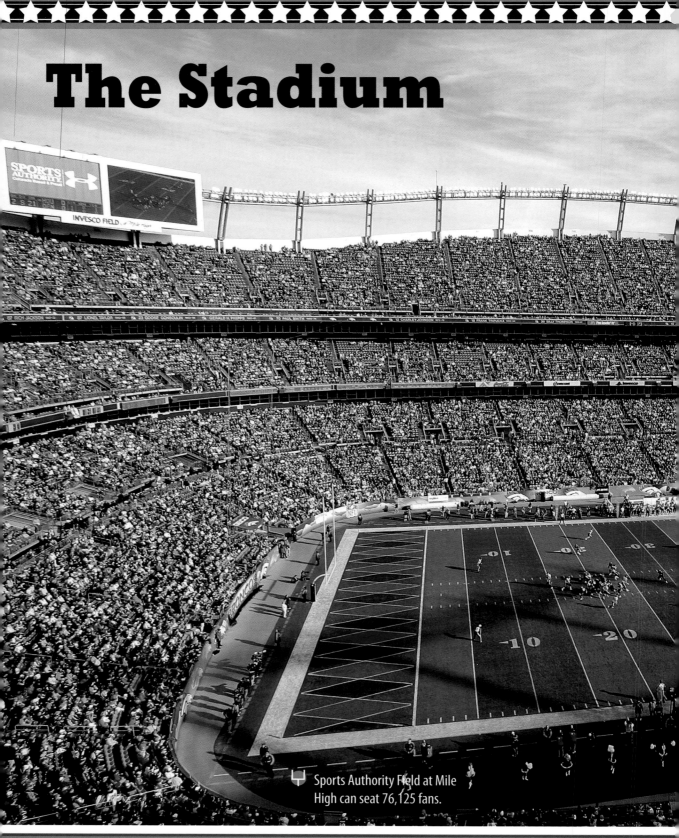

Sports Authority Field at Mile High can seat 76,125 fans.

Sports Authority Field at Mile High rests on the same grounds as the legendary Mile High Stadium, home to the Denver Broncos from 1960 until 2001. Since opening in 2001, the tradition of sellouts in Denver has continued at Sports Authority. The Broncos have sold out every game they have played at their current stadium.

Denver Broncos fans show their "Broncomania" when they dress up for home games.

Named "Mile High" because Denver is roughly 1 mile (1.6 kilometers) above sea level, Sports Authority Field can be tough on visiting players. The air gets thinner as the **altitude** gets higher, so people need to work harder to breathe. Players who are not used to high altitudes tire quickly. By combining less oxygen, a wild crowd, and the excellent Broncos, Sports Authority Field is one of the least popular destinations for NFL teams.

Sports Authority Field also has many other uses. The stadium hosts college football games, Major League Lacrosse games, rock concerts, and conventions. In 2008, Barack Obama accepted the Democratic Party's presidential nomination in front of a crowd of 84,000 people at Sports Authority Field.

Sports Authority Field offers hungry fans a wide range of delectable items, from hot dogs and polish sausages to burritos, pizza, tamales, and grilled chicken sandwiches.

Where They Play

CANADA

Washington

Oregon

Montana

North Dakota

Minnesota

Lake Superior

Idaho

South Dakota

Wisconsin

Nevada

Wyoming

Iowa

Illinois

California

Utah

Colorado

Nebraska

Missouri

UNITED STATES

Arizona

New Mexico

Kansas

Oklahoma

Arkansas

Pacific Ocean

Texas

Mississippi

Louisiana

Gulf of Mexico

Alaska

0   500 Miles
0   500 km

Hawai'i

0   100 Miles
0   100 km

MEXICO

AMERICAN FOOTBALL CONFERENCE

EAST	NORTH	SOUTH	WEST
1 Gillette Stadium	5 FirstEnergy Stadium	9 EverBank Field	13 Arrowhead Stadium
2 MetLife Stadium	6 Heinz Field	10 LP Field	14 Sports Authority Field at Mile High
3 Ralph Wilson Stadium	7 M&T Bank Stadium	11 Lucas Oil Stadium	15 O.co Coliseum
4 Sun Life Stadium	8 Paul Brown Stadium	12 NRG Stadium	16 Qualcomm Stadium

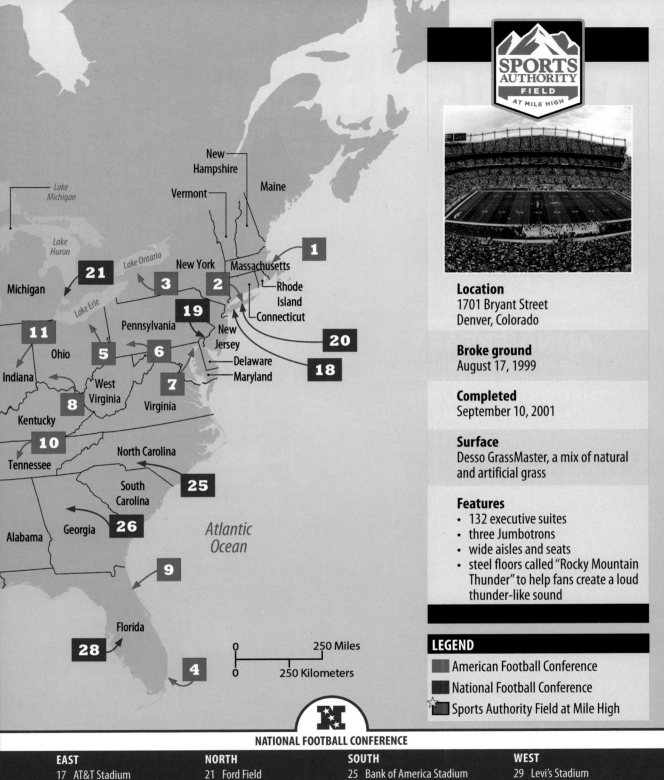

SPORTS AUTHORITY FIELD AT MILE HIGH

Location
1701 Bryant Street
Denver, Colorado

Broke ground
August 17, 1999

Completed
September 10, 2001

Surface
Desso GrassMaster, a mix of natural and artificial grass

Features
- 132 executive suites
- three Jumbotrons
- wide aisles and seats
- steel floors called "Rocky Mountain Thunder" to help fans create a loud thunder-like sound

LEGEND
- American Football Conference
- National Football Conference
- Sports Authority Field at Mile High

NATIONAL FOOTBALL CONFERENCE

EAST	NORTH	SOUTH	WEST
17 AT&T Stadium	21 Ford Field	25 Bank of America Stadium	29 Levi's Stadium
18 FedExField	22 Lambeau Field	26 Georgia Dome	30 CenturyLink Field
19 Lincoln Financial Field	23 Mall of America Field	27 Mercedes-Benz Superdome	31 Edward Jones Dome
20 MetLife Stadium	24 Soldier Field	28 Raymond James Stadium	★ 32 University of Phoenix Stadium

The Uniforms

To celebrate their
—— **50**th ——
ANNIVERSARY
in 2009, the Broncos
wore yellow and brown
"THROWBACK"UNIFORMS
against the Patriots.

 Denver recognizes 23 past players and administrators in their Ring of Fame, an area in the stadium where these famous names are on display.

With the Broncos struggling in their first few seasons of play, people paid more attention to the uniforms than the team. Featuring white and mustard yellow jerseys, brown helmets, brown pants, and vertically striped socks, they are commonly referred to as the ugliest uniforms in the history of professional football. These uniforms were replaced in 1962 by white pants, orange helmets, and either orange or white jerseys.

Today, the main color on the Broncos' home jersey is orange, with their navy blue jerseys being used only as an **alternate jersey**. White pants are worn for both home and road games.

Football uniforms have changed over time to become tougher and more elastic, giving players a greater range of motion.

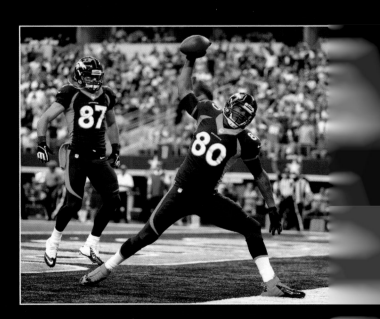

The Helmets

A HORSE, OF COURSE

The Broncos' current helmet logo is a profile of a horse's head with orange mane and navy blue outlines.

NFL helmet designs have changed over time to improve player safety. Modern helmets are made from lightweight plastic shells that are very tough.

In 1962, the Broncos moved on from their mustard yellow jersey and brown helmet uniforms. The new helmets were orange with a blue bucking bronco. Except for small color changes, the helmet stayed the same until 1967, when it was replaced with a blue helmet with an orange-white-orange stripe down the center.

In 1968, the helmet was redesigned to feature an uppercase "D" with a snorting, bucking bronco in the middle of the letter. With this logo on the sides of their helmets, the Broncos changed their national image, growing from a weak franchise into one of the league's best.

At the start of the 1997 season, the Broncos replaced their blue helmets with a navy blue helmet and a "swift" orange Bronco logo. Soon afterward, they won their first Super Bowl, and the quest for a better logo ended. Since 1997, the only thing about the helmets that has changed is the shade of blue.

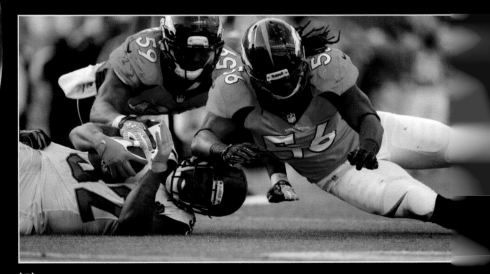

Without proper safety gear, football can be a very dangerous sport. Helmets, as well as leg and shoulder pads, help keep players safe.

The Coaches

13 John Fox recorded back-to-back 13-win regular seasons in 2012 and 2013 as the head coach of the Denver Broncos.

John Fox began his coaching career in 1978 as a graduate assistant at San Diego State University.

Since the Broncos were formed, 14 different head coaches have paced the Denver sideline. In total, Denver's coaches have earned six Coach of the Year awards. The first man to win the award was former college football star Red Miller. Under Miller's guidance, the Broncos grew from a good team with a great defense into an NFL powerhouse that played in their first of six Super Bowls. Miller started a pattern of great leadership that remains to this day.

DAN REEVES

An injury to Dan Reeves' knee in 1969 made him slower, and reduced his role on the Dallas Cowboys' offense. In 1981, the Broncos hired Reeves to be their new head coach, making him the youngest head coach in the NFL. In 12 years, Reeves led the Broncos to 110 wins, six division titles, and three AFC Championships.

MIKE SHANAHAN

Shanahan favored a run-heavy version of the **"West Coast" offense**. The system worked like a charm, with six different Broncos' running backs gaining more than 1,000 yards in a season over a 10-year span. Shanahan's two Super Bowl wins are the only championships by any Broncos' coach.

JOHN FOX

In three seasons with the Broncos, Fox coached the team to three straight AFC West division titles and the 2013 AFC Championship. Hopes remain high that Fox will bring the team their third Super Bowl title in 2014.

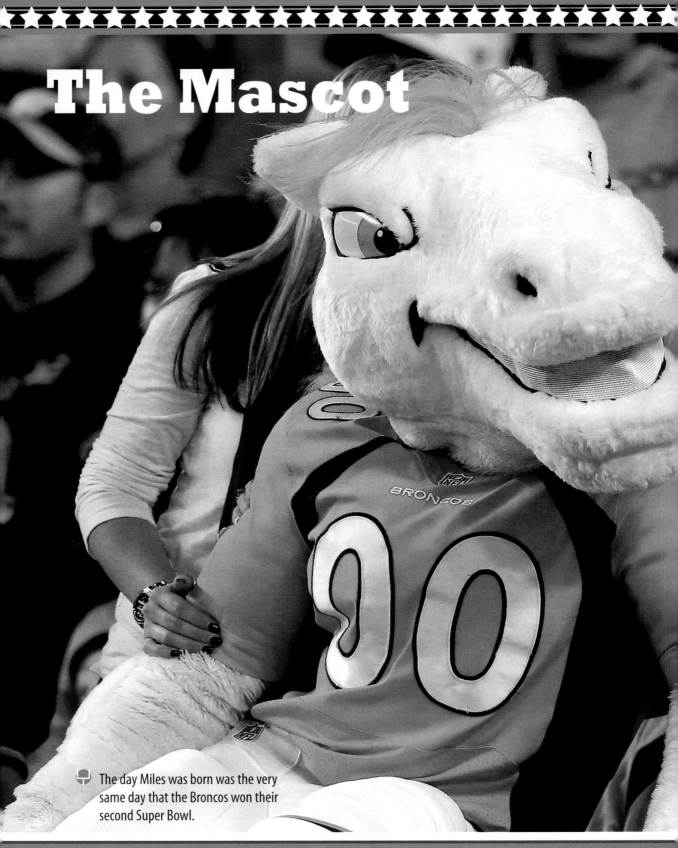

The Mascot

The day Miles was born was the very same day that the Broncos won their second Super Bowl.

On January 31, 1999, a bolt of lightning split the Denver sky and Miles the mascot was born. Raised high up in the Rocky Mountains, far above the city of Denver and Mile High, a herd of wild horses taught Miles two things: how to be a good horse and how to be a good fan of the Denver Broncos. Miles got the message loud and clear.

In 2001, entranced by the sight of a distant field that looked perfect for grazing, Miles migrated to the city. That field turned out to be none other than Sports Authority Field at Mile High. Miles could not believe his luck. From that day forward, he took up his spot on the sideline and vowed to be the best mascot he could be.

The Broncos have another mascot named "Thunder." He is a purebred Arabian gelding who has been galloping the sidelines since 2004.

In addition to leading the cheers at Broncos' games, Miles makes appearances for the literacy program "Read Like a Pro."

Legends of the Past

Many great players have suited up in the Broncos' orange and navy. A few of them have become icons of the team and the city it represents.

Shannon Sharpe

Shannon Sharpe was the first NFL tight end to surpass 10,000 receiving yards in his career. His consistently high level of play in the 1990s helped to form championship teams in Denver. Sharpe was a leader in the locker room as well as on the field. In 1997, Sharpe led the team in receptions (72) en route to their first Super Bowl victory, and in 1998, he led the team in receiving touchdowns (10). Over the course of his career, Sharpe made six Pro Bowls and was a four-time All Pro. He was inducted into the Pro Football Hall of Fame in 2011.

Position Tight End
Seasons 14 (1990–2003)
Born June 26, 1968, in Chicago, Illinois

Champ Bailey

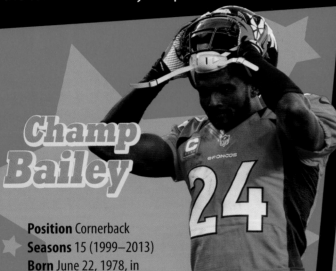

Position Cornerback
Seasons 15 (1999–2013)
Born June 22, 1978, in Folkston, Georgia

Champ Bailey was regarded by many as one of the best pass defenders in NFL history. He ranked first among all Broncos with 52 interceptions, 34 of those coming with Denver. A football and a track and field star at the University of Georgia, Bailey used his blazing speed and great leaping ability to cover opposing wide receivers and earn an NFL cornerback-record 12 invitations to the Pro Bowl.

While Bailey maintained a high level of play throughout his career, his finest season may have come in 2005, when he intercepted 10 passes and did not allow a single touchdown.

John Elway

Following the 1983 NFL Draft, in which the winless Baltimore Colts drafted Elway with the first overall pick, Elway considered playing baseball for the New York Yankees. However, when the Colts agreed to trade him to Denver, Elway settled on football and went on to rewrite the Broncos' record books. During his 15-year career, John Elway appeared in nine Pro Bowls and five Super Bowls. After winning two straight championships in 1997 and 1998, he was named MVP of Super Bowl XXXIII in 1998.

Position Quarterback
Seasons 15 (1983–1998)
Born June 28, 1960, in Port Angeles, Washington

Terrell Davis

In Terrell Davis' first four seasons in the NFL, he rushed for 6,413 yards and 56 touchdowns. His total yardage through four NFL seasons was the third most among modern-era hall of fame running backs, and his 56 touchdowns topped them all. Davis' most memorable performance came in the 1997 Super Bowl. During the big game, he rushed for 157 yards and was named the game's **Most Valuable Player (MVP)**. He accomplished this despite having missed the entire second quarter with a very painful headache. In 1998, Davis became the fourth running back in league history to rush for more than 2,000 yards in a single season.

Position Running Back
Seasons 7 (1995–2002)
Born October 28, 1972, in San Diego, California

Stars of Today

Today's Broncos team is made up of many young, talented players who have proven that they are among the best players in the league.

Peyton Manning

Peyton Manning was a living legend long before he came to Mile High. When he arrived in Denver, however, the future hall of fame quarterback still had plenty of goals left to accomplish. One of them was to show that he could recover from neck surgery and retake his place at the top of the NFL. In 2012, four-time MVP Peyton Manning put up his best statistical season since 2004, throwing for 4,659 yards and 37 touchdowns. In 2013, he topped those numbers, averaging more than 300 passing yards per game and recording one of the greatest statistical seasons in NFL history.

Position Quarterback
Seasons 16 (1998–2013)
Born March 24, 1976, in New Orleans, Louisiana

Von Miller

In the 2012 season, Von Miller set the Denver Broncos' single-season **sacks** record with 18.5, forced six fumbles, and recorded 56 quarterback hurries. He was second in the voting for NFL Defensive Player of the Year, cementing his reputation as one of the league's great young defenders.

Von Miller's success came as no surprise to anyone who had paid attention to his college career. At Texas A&M University, Miller led the nation with 17 sacks in his junior season. As a senior, he won the **Butkus Award** for nation's best linebacker.

Position Linebacker
Seasons 3 (2011–2013)
Born March 26, 1989, in Dallas, Texas

DeMarcus Ware

DeMarcus Ware's ability to play defensive end as well as linebacker has earned him the unofficial label of "most dynamic defender in the league." In 2012, he became just the third player in NFL history to register 10 or more sacks in seven straight seasons and was selected to play in his seventh straight Pro Bowl. In Denver, this two-time Butkus Award winner who has led the NFL in sacks twice, will team up with Von Miller to form one of the scariest pass rushing duos in the NFL.

Position Defensive End
Seasons 9 (2005–2013)
Born July 31, 1982, in Auburn, Alabama

Demaryius Thomas

Demaryius Thomas got off to a quick start in the NFL. In his first game, he recorded eight receptions for 97 yards. While much of his rookie season was hampered by injuries, the Broncos' coaching staff was well aware that they might have something special in Thomas. When Peyton Manning came to the Broncos, he commented on Thomas' size, strength, and speed, saying that those qualities allowed him to do things on the field that other receivers could not hope to do. In two seasons with Manning, Thomas has put his athletic gifts to good use, registering more than 2,800 receiving yards and 24 receiving touchdowns.

Position Wide Receiver
Seasons 4 (2010–2013)
Born December 25, 1987, in Montrose, Georgia

All-Time Records

97.5
Career Sacks

Simon Fletcher tormented opposing offenses in the 1980s and 1990s, registering 97.5 sacks in 11 seasons with Denver.

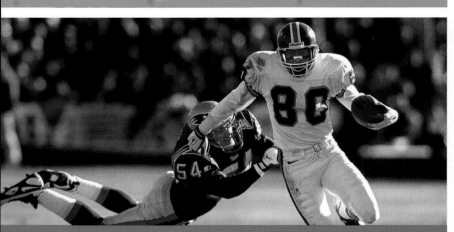

11,389 Career Receiving Yards

Rod Smith registered more than 1,000 receiving yards eight times in his brilliant 12-year career.

60 Career Rushing Touchdowns

Terrell Davis earned the nickname "T.D." by rushing for 56 touchdowns in his first four seasons and 60 in his career.

51,475

Career Passing Yards

No other Denver quarterback comes close to John Elway's career passing yardage. His career total is good for fourth best on the NFL's all-time list.

4,659 Single-season Passing Yards

In his first season with the Broncos in 1998, Peyton Manning set the club's all-time record for passing yards in a single season.

Timeline

Throughout the team's history, the Denver Broncos have had many memorable events that have become defining moments for the team and its fans.

1962
New head coach Jack Faulkner ritualistically burns the Broncos brown and yellow uniforms and the Broncos change their colors to orange, royal blue, and white. All Pro wide receiver Lionel Taylor and professional football's first African American placekicker Gene Mingo lead Denver to its first **.500 season**.

1967
Head coach Lou Saban drafts three-time **All-American** Floyd Little. Little and other Broncos players go door-to-door in Colorado, Wyoming, and Nebraska in order to raise enough money to save the franchise.

In 1978, the Broncos face the Dallas Cowboys in Super Bowl XII, but lose the game 27-10.

| 1960 | 1965 | 1970 | 1975 | 1980 | 1985 |

December 9, 1960
The AFL begins its **inaugural** season. Frank Tripucka and Al Carmichael shine for the Denver Broncos, as they beat the Boston Patriots 13-10 in the franchise's first game.

1970
The AFL and the NFL merge. The Broncos are placed in the AFC West. They sell out every single home game, beginning a run of sellouts that continues to this day.

1983
After 23 years in which the Broncos use 24 different quarterbacks, John Elway arrives in Denver, bringing the team stability and leadership. The Broncos finish the season 9-7 and the future looks bright.

January 25, 1998

The Broncos ride the NFL's best offense all the way to Super Bowl XXXII, where they face Brett Favre and the heavily favored Green Bay Packers. Despite suffering from a terrible headache, Terrell Davis rushes for 157 yards and leads the Broncos to their first Super Bowl win.

The Future

With Peyton Manning at the helm, the 2013 Denver Broncos had the best offense in the NFL. Manning broke the single-season records for passing yards (5,477) and passing touchdowns (55). In 2014, with the addition of Pro Bowlers DeMarcus Ware and Aqib Talib, Von Miller and the revitalized Denver defense will look to be as dominant as their teammates on offense. The Broncos may have fallen just short of a championship in 2013, but their Super Bowl hopes remain mile high.

In 2005, the Broncos win the AFC West for the first time since Elway's retirement.

| 1990 | 1995 | 2000 | 2005 | 2010 | 2015 |

In 1996, Terrell Davis and Shannon Sharpe shine as Denver has its most dynamic offensive attack in years.

1987

After a disappointing loss in Super Bowl XXI, Elway and linebacker Karl Mecklenburg rally Denver to another division crown. Elway is named NFL MVP, and the Broncos advance to another Super Bowl. In Super Bowl XXII, Denver takes a 10-0 lead, but Washington scores 35 second-quarter points and wins the game.

2012

In his first season back from neck surgery, Peyton Manning guides the Broncos to a 13-3 record, an AFC West division title, and is named NFL Comeback Player of the Year. The Broncos suffer a heartbreaking loss to Baltimore in the divisional round of the playoffs.

Write a Biography

Life Story

A person's life story can be the subject of a book. This kind of book is called a biography. Biographies often describe the lives of people who have achieved great success. These people may be alive today, or they may have lived many years ago. Reading a biography can help you learn more about a great person.

Get the Facts

Use this book, and research in the library and on the Internet, to find out more about your favorite Bronco. Learn as much about this player as you can. What position does he play? What are his statistics in important categories? Has he set any records? Also, be sure to write down key events in the person's life. What was his childhood like? What has he accomplished off the field? Is there anything else that makes this person special or unusual?

Use the Concept Web

A concept web is a useful research tool. Read the questions in the concept web on the following page. Answer the questions in your notebook. Your answers will help you write a biography.

Concept Web

Adulthood
- Where does this individual currently reside?
- Does he or she have a family?

Your Opinion
- What did you learn from the books you read in your research?
- Would you suggest these books to others?
- Was anything missing from these books?

Childhood
- Where and when was this person born?
- Describe his or her parents, siblings, and friends.
- Did this person grow up in unusual circumstances?

Accomplishments off the Field
- What is this person's life's work?
- Has he or she received awards or recognition for accomplishments?
- How have this person's accomplishments served others?

Write a Biography

Help and Obstacles
- Did this individual have a positive attitude?
- Did he or she receive help from others?
- Did this person have a mentor?
- Did this person face any hardships?
- If so, how were the hardships overcome?

Accomplishments on the Field
- What records does this person hold?
- What key games and plays have defined his or her career?
- What are his or her stats in categories important to his or her position?

Work and Preparation
- What was this person's education?
- What was his or her work experience?
- How does this person work; what is the process he or she uses?

Trivia Time

Take this quiz to test your knowledge of the Denver Broncos. The answers are printed upside-down under each question.

1 Which Broncos running back was nicknamed "The Franchise"?

A. Floyd Little

2 How many Broncos players have been inducted into the Pro Football Hall of Fame?

A. Four

3 In what year did the Broncos first qualify for the playoffs?

A. 1977

4 What was the nickname of the 1977 Broncos defense that led the team to Super Bowl XII?

A. "Orange Crush"

5 What year did the Broncos home sellout streak begin?

A. 1970

6 In what season was John Elway named NFL MVP?

A. 1998

7 Who was the MVP of 1997 Super Bowl XXXII, the Broncos' first of back-to-back championships?

A. Terrell Davis

8 What are the names of the Broncos' two mascots?

A. Miles and Thunder

9 How many AFC titles have the Broncos won?

A. Six

10 What was the name given to the steel floors at Sports Authority Field at Mile High?

A. "Rocky Mountain Thunder"

Key Words

.500 season: when a team wins and loses an equal number of games. In the NFL, an 8-8 record constitutes a .500 season

All-American: a player, usually in high school or college, judged to be the best in each position of a sport

All Pro: a term used to designate the best players of each position during a given season

alternate jersey: a jersey that sports teams may wear in games instead of their home or away uniforms

altitude: the height of an object or place in relation to sea level or ground level

American Football League (AFL): the American Football League (AFL) was a major American Professional Football league that operated from 1960 until 1969, when it merged with the National Football League (NFL)

Butkus Award: named for hall of fame linebacker Dick Butkus, this award is given annually to the top linebackers at the high school, collegiate, and professional levels of football

charter members: original or founding members of an organization

hall of fame: a group of persons judged to be outstanding, as in a sport or profession

inaugural: marking the beginning of an institution, activity, or period of office

logo: a symbol that stands for a team or organization

Most Valuable Player (MVP): the player judged to be most valuable to his team's success

Pro Bowler: an NFL player who takes part in the annual all-star game that pits the best players in the National Football Conference against the best players in the American Football Conference

sacks: when the quarterback, or another offensive player acting as a passer, is tackled behind the line of scrimmage before he can throw a forward pass

Super Bowl: the NFL's annual championship game between the winning team from the NFC and the winning team from the AFC

"West Coast" offense: the offensive system popularized by Bill Walsh, characterized by short, horizontal passing routes used to "stretch out" defenses, opening up the potential for long runs or long passes

Index

Log on to www.av2books.com

AV² by Weigl brings you media enhanced books that support active learning. Go to www.av2books.com, and enter the special code found on page 2 of this book. You will gain access to enriched and enhanced content that supplements and complements this book. Content includes video, audio, weblinks, quizzes, a slide show, and activities.

AV² Online Navigation

Book Pages
AV² pages directly correspond to pages in the book.

Audio
Listen to sections of the book read aloud.

Video
Watch informative video clips.

Embedded Weblinks
Gain additional information for research.

Key Words
Study vocabulary, and complete a matching word activity.

Try This!
Complete activities and hands-on experiments.

Quizzes
Test your knowledge.

Slide Show
View images and captions, and prepare a presentation.

AV² was built to bridge the gap between print and digital. We encourage you to tell us what you like and what you want to see in the future.

Sign up to be an AV² Ambassador at www.av2books.com/ambassador.